# SUNLIGHT ON A SQUARE

# BASIL PAYNE

Published by C. Payne, 2015

ISBN 978-0-9931658-0-1

# CHILD AND MAN . . .

# THE CULPRITS

First it was death: my grandfather
Stretched cold in bed one Sunday afternoon,
Pennies -gold pennies- resting on his eyes,
Made Sunday different; next day, consoled,
By adult lies and bribes, I travelled gleefully
Beside the driver on a horse-drawn cab,
And ate a Currant bun while Mother wept;
-Still, I remembered. Later, it was love
Deceived: a girl who laughed and tossed
My golden-penny phrases in my face,
raced away to play with her companions;
This time, for a full day I did not eat.

Life hardens; other deaths and other passion
Followed, and were confronted in a fashion
As befits an adult: by distraction.
Distracted from distraction by distraction.
Recording childhood's anguish can dispense
Comfort of sorts for ingrown common-sense.

# LANDMARKS

Recalling childhood, houses are the most
Decisive landmarks; first, a red brick house
Near the canal, where, giggling and afraid,
We went to see a classmate's father, dead
And dressed in brown; his mother pouring out
Weak lemonade in breakfast cups; a cat
Stealing the milk from an enormous jug.
Next, a slaughter-house in Harold's Cross,
Where two of us at lunch-time watched a man,
Red-faced, with rubber boots and bloody hands,
Kill with a. spike a lean bedraggled sheep,
which bleated only once, but twitched long after.
Lastly, a white-washed house near Dolphin's Barn,
Where, it was rumoured, lived, alone, a witch.
I saw her Once: a. woman dressed in black,
With massive ankles; hobbling to the yard
Outside, she shook an apron-full of crumbs,
Or something, to her hens; then, seeing us,
Shouted "clearoff, clear off, you little brats!"
Running away, I tripped and cut my knee,
And heard her mumble dreadful, dreadful things.

# RECOLLECTIONS

## I.— Mrs. Williams

"Send for Mrs. Williams," young wives said,;
Sweating in labour in big double bed;
 And gladly, guiltily, husbands fled
For ever-ready midwife Mrs. Williams.
"Send for Mrs. Williams," old folk said,
Saying their Beads at old folks' death-beds;
And gladly, guiltily young folk sped
For corpse-washing and corpse-laying Mrs. Williams.
She died, herself, at eighty, one raw day
In March; small children playing in the street
Gathered to watch a half-a-dozen neighbours
Follow the tiny-coffined last remains
Of larger-than-life-or-judgment Mrs. Williams.

## II.— Mad Larry

Mad Larry gripped me by the arm
So tightly that I cried; then asked
"Who's going to win the match?" "Why, Rovers!"
I shouted wildly; "Rovers! Rovers!"
—Eyeing the emblem on his coat lapel,
And spit-stained muffler wound about his neck.
Grinning, he let me go, and gave me
A caramel wrapped in dirty silver paper.
Looking behind me as I ran away,
I saw him capturing another boy.

## III.—Mr. and Mrs. Isaac's

Mr. and Mm. Isaac lived at number ten.

They'd fled from Hitler; both spoke awkward English,
Yet managed nicely on their modest business:
Hairdressing — with a money-lending sideline.
Unlicensed, and with prosecution pending,
The neighbours found them gassed, their windows sealed
Against their worse-than-Auschwitz Irish Judas.

## IV. —The Misses Anderson

Miss Susan and Miss Adelaide,
Two thin-faced ageing sisters, frayed
By loneliness, sharp-eyed as rats,
Bestowed their narrow love on cats,
A parrot and a mongrel bitch.
Susan, Ada — which was which
None of us could rightly say;
They never passed the time-of-day
With us; a skinny hand came out
Each night to leave milk bottles out.

# ANGRY OLD MEN

Those days, the angry persons were the old:
Killarny, for instance (so we christened him),
An old man with a long and yellow beard,
Who, at exactly two each Tuesday,
Sang By Killarny's Lakes:
outside our house father often set his watch by him.
-He never knocked for alms; but roared abuse
And shook his walking-stick at us, when we
Mocked him with our soprano schoolboy chorus:
Until, one Tuesday, he did not turn up:
-None of us ever heard what happened him.

Next, there was Damn the Weather; less predictable
Than old Killarncy, and more violent;
He would come stamping down the street in boots
A size too big for him, and leather leggings
-A swearing, one-man army on the march.
Winter or summer, purple-faced, shout
"Damn the weather; damn the bloody weather!"
-"Shell-shock," my mother patiently explained.

The Blind Man came on Sundays: him alone
The rules secured from children's mockery.
I did not like him; pounding on each door
Aggressively, he'd order "Help the Blind!",
Adding "God Bless You," when he got his coin.
(None of our parents ever dared refuse).

# LINES IN MEMORY OF MY FATHER

Fishing, one morning early in July
From the canal bank —that was the closest ever
We came to entering each other's world;
That, and one wintry day at the Museum,
Looking at ancient coins and skeletons,
Dead butterflies, old guns and stones;
Each of us slightly awed, and slightly bored,
And slightly uneasy at each other's boredom.
I cried, of course, the morning that you died,
Frightened by Mother's tears and your grey spittle,
 And frightened at being suddenly bereft
Of someone I had never loved enough,
But vaguely understood had loved me.

To-day in Dublin, passing the Museum,
A dead leaf blew across my instep, stabbing
My memory suddenly: little frightened fishes
Flapping bewildered in a cheap white net,
Then gliding in a water-filled jam jar;
Nudging their awkward heads against the glass.
Groping in vain for green and spacious freedom.

# FATHER AND SON

Sorrow, like snow in April, merely hoods
Established growth or habit: after grief,
The hare and chastened mind shakes off its brief
Encounter with the absolute, the edge
Of rugged reason, jaggedly emerging,
Punctures sap, intrepidly converging
Sunshine, and frantic foliage, and knowledge
Of tendril gropings somewhere in dull roots.

Only the child, intact in its intense
And pure communion with experience,
Sees through its grief the enemy's white face,
The evil restitution can't displace:
The broken toy, the confiscated comic,
The sapling's sudden foretaste of the tragic.

# MAN ALONE . . .

# PROMETHEUS

An angry seagull, with a raucous voice
Screamed his indignant disappointment,
At six this morning, when he found T
he object he'd mistaken for a crust
Was but a white mark on my window-sill.
And as he paused too proud to fy away
Immediately, no spoils to brag about
We eyed each other, silently.
He, alert and poised,
But with defiance in his beady eyes,
And I, still dim-eyed, glazed with sleep,
Admiring (half-grudgingly, because he woke me up)
His Shell-white, glossy breast,
Smooth and immaculate
As nun's starched linen. . . .
Suddenly, with a short derisive yell,
A great disdainful flap of outstretched wings,
Swift as a guiltless soul, he sped
Into the turquoise chastity
Of early-morning skies.
Then, with a sigh, I turned upon my side,
ans parachuted gently
Back to the hooded safety of sleep.

Grey rain was falling from a ragged sky
When I awoke

# THE WRECKERS

It is the small betrayals that betray
The solemn Great Betrayal, hovering
With helicopter cunning in the crisp
Skies of inconsequential subterfuge,
Above the flotsam of our scuttled lives.
Always the same: the s.o.s. of doubt;
The glib mind tapping out the clichéd lie;
The garbled phrase; the riveted excuse
For imminent premeditated failure;
While still the furnaces of falsehood solder
The twisted girders of the soul's dismay.
Until the last deceit: the rescue-craft
Of whirring evil, dangling rope-end wiles
To jerk us from our foundering despair
To cockpits of unbounded unreality.

# CROSSING THE BARRIER

Flight is the catchword: only to penetrate
Time-honoured barriers of remote restraint
Urges us onwards, anxious to integrate
Whirlwind endeavour with the still complaint
Of individual loneliness, or disappear
In tail-spins of twin-engined fame and fear.

O brave new world that is no longer brave,
The siren sounds: don't vacillate between
Soul-splintering flight from time's uncharted spleen
And slow driftwood of ennui on the wave.
Stir from the surface, dip from the greedy skies,
And jettison your fears —the Absolute
Still canopies your truant enterprise;
Venture the valour that you now refute.

# RALLY FOR PEACE IN TRAFALGAR SQUARE

*(1st July, 1961)*

The genial camouflaging sun
Smears the stream with happiness
—A cynic might begin this way,
A cynic with sharp things to say
About this sunny English lease
Of life: vague meetings preaching peace
From wooden platforms to a crowd
Of hot, perspiring tourists, loud-
Ly laughing at the pigeons' antics,
Snap-happy Kodachrome Romantics,
Equipped with Miniature, Reflex,
Ciné or simple Box; complex
Emotions tightly stored-up, ready
For Future exhibition . . . steady!
Is 'going tourist', then, a crime
Peculiar to the non-sublime?
A tour de force of innocence
Abroad? a sturdy recompense
For stunted sensibility?
Or is it an agility
Of spirit, gravitating towards
Platforms of love? applause at Lords
Or Wimbledon; the lusty roar
Of Wembley; thrills and spills galore,
Allaying unremitting life -
Sentences to boss - or wife -
Or husband-servitude; the dour,

Slow handclap for the matador,
Who, lunging at the sentenced bull,
Fails and fails again to kill.

Yet, all are killers; killing time
In drinking, checkers, sex or rhyme;
Shooting crap to our connections,
Taking murderous directions
on family-planning; what to eat;
How to be successful; meet
The proper people; cultivate
An air of tolerance, when hate
Enables us to make a just
Man bite the just-consuming dust.
Let's face it: killing is a game
Indulged in mostly as a lame
Alternative to living; youth-
Ful exhortations about truth
Are okay, but you've got to lie
In ambush for survival. (My
Own conscience, you will understand,
Is equally uneasy: bland
Rhyming couplet don't command
A primogeniture of peace,
Or give a special kind of lease
To falsehood; lies most cunning terse-
Ly masquerade as truth in verse).

## II

But on this gay and golden afternoon,
There's no denying peace is all around me.
It dawdles by the fountains, where schoolgirls
In yellow blouses giggle eagerly
At nothing; small boys splash and lovers flick

The waters with clasped hands. Nelson, aloft,
Reclines against blue skies which clearly augur Perpetual peace for
all. Trafalgar's ghost
Is laid. Trafalgar is not cannon's smoke,
Death-shriek or mangled leg from musket-ball.

### III

Trafalgar is tame pigeons futtering
Obediently to hand or shoulder; tall
Africans in silken garments taking
Each others photographs; small Englishmen
In shirt-sleeves risking sunburn. Such fulfilment
Is purer stuff than speeches: Isolate
This moment, stranger; store it for your friends' Consideration;
universal claptrap
On co-existence will not alter this:
Peace can't be consummated by a kiss.

# LINES FOR A LIBERTINE

His maiden voyage was scheduled, if bemused,
The maiden compliant, the gay dog gay;
His heart's horizon boundless and diffused,
He'd scour the seven seas of lively prey
—Self-ordinate, he pondered, seeing his victims walk
The plank of tapered lust and facile talk.

Currents of chill regrets clutch at the wreck
Of jettisoned affections, foundered hopes,
And gummed-reefed betrayals; no last trek
To port of sheltered virtue; no stray tug
Of love or shafted intellect to lug
This hulk of doomed, disintegrating passion
That frisked life's foam, derided all compassion:
Alone, he waits the vortex that will bed
His ravaged frame with his penumbral dread.

# ON KEITA FODEBA'S AFRICAN DANCERS

Mysterious mortality, like shaking Orange-blossom,
Urged by unfathomed rhythms jungle cannot enfold,
Leaps into foaming ecstasy, triumphantly transcending
Earth's supine immobility; soon, soon the marigold
Fecundity of nature seduces mortal glory;
Beat loud, beat proud, O dark drums, tell your primeval
                                        story:

Beat in the midnight's thicket the quintessential bravery
Of Kamambourema, or vibrantly disguise
The elemental treachery of stillness: the sad slavery
Of lovers, chaste as moonlight, plucking order from the skies.
"Earth and water, fire and air, are reality; despair
Will sap the febrile fervour from the thought-tormented
                                        bone."
"Death ?"—"Death is final ecstasy!" O drums, where is
                              your laughter?
Must your lofty gods' remoteness leave the dancers so alone?

# THE FOREST

It is dark in the forest.
Man, shiny with sweat,
Slough through the vapid undergrowth
Grunt and beget.

Beget not dreams nor progeny,
Nor even bastard-thought:
Disseminated loneliness
Is dearly bought.

Beget bedevilled consciousness
Of a discarded vision,
Snared in a noose of sunlit prayer,
Strangled by indecision.

Strangled by evil shadows
Snatching a golden find
From the forsaken forest
Of a man's mind.

It is dark in the forest;
The drums of madness throbbing
In the distended midnight
Set the heart sobbing.

# EXISTENTIAL ECSTASIES

Patients before a bloody major op.
Premeditated, will not order "stop!"

Conscripts advancing in a shell-lit sky
Are decorated maybe; maybe die.

Hoboes and tramps united in division,
Squat in abandoned outposts of decision.

Poets prospecting on a vacant site
Reject the spark to set themselves alight.

Old men exploring for lost innocence
Impale themselves on second-childhood's fence

Children, protective innocence unfurled,
Trail with the flotsam of the adult world.

Importunate, imprisoned in earth's pod,
Dreading the liberating rays of God;
Defining and declining being; i.e.
Essential existential ecstasy.

# THE HANGED MAN

*(Freely translated from the German of Stefan George)*

## THE QUESTIONER:

You, from the gallows now cut free,
What have you to say to me?

## THE HANGED MAN:

When, fouling the air with their crude shouts
And curses, the capricious louts
Dragged me to the town's gates, then
I saw in these crime-hating men
— Stonethrowers, and those other curs
With folded arms who wrought the spurs
Of hatred for their neighbours' use,
Pointing long fingers of abuse
At me - I saw in each wild eye
A diabolic, crusted lie:
Latent in each, hemmed in by fear
One of my sins lurked, narrower
Than mine, but every bit as real
—Evil impressed with virtue's seal.

When, at the gallows, shortly after
They stood, I was convulsed with laughter
At the stern schizophrenic faces
Of justice pulling at its traces;
Disgust and pity wrangling
Over my shabby dangling.
"Crackpotsl" I cried, "which is the winner,
Upright virtue? downcast sinner?
Madmen! do you not realise

True virtue must be sinner-wise?"
Virtue - against which I'd offended —
Shone in their upturned faces, blended
With fear; but virtue, however real,
Would not have quite the same appeal,
Nor glow on face of decent wife
Or girl, if my poor sinful life
Did not provide the contrast: Sin
Both formulates and boosts unsin.
When they put my neck into the noose,
My malice drew from my abuse
This furtive triumph: I, the hanged,
Defeated one, will be the fanged
Conqueror who storms your brains,
And puts your guilty souls in chains.
And I'll be active in your seed
As any hero there conceived,
About whom songs are sung . . . A God ...
I'll bend, and bend, this stiffened rod
Into a wheel, before you've time
To snatch it from the burning lime.

# CATS

*(Translated from the French of Charles Baudelaire)*

Austere men-of-learning, hot-blooded men of passion,
Lavish the same affection (growing discreetly old)
On cats (discreetly absolute); idols of the household;
Draught-sensitive and sedentary, in their owners' fashion.

Friends alike of learning and of sensuality,
They probe night's dreadful darkness, the silence of the tomb
Erebus might employ them as messengers of gloom,
Could they forgo their proud, recalcitrant duality.

Relaxing, they assume the meditative pose
Of mighty sphinxes stretching their limbs in bland repose;
Solitary, slumbering in an endless dream.

Magic sparkles darkly in their fertile loins
Eye-pupils, vaguely star-Hecked, mysteriously gleam,
Fine-particled as sand-grains, hard as golden coins.

# SUNLIGHT ON A SQUARE

*(Anniversary lines for James Joyce, born Brighton Square, Rathgar, Dublin, February 2, 1882)*

This brittle, sun-daubed February day,
Dangling the treacherous Golden Fleece of spring,
Impinges on the memory the stark,
Attenuated kinship of tall trees,
Exiled of song and leaf, yet obdurate;
The rugged sentinels of buried genius,
Begotten on the humble, terraced base
Of this green-parked, isosceles triangle,
Miscalled, by public arrogance, a "Square".
This, then, his dogged, desiccating task:
To spurn the fixed triangle, and extend
Imagination's landmarks; making limitless
The limits of transacting dialectics:
The sad, compelling landscape of the conscious;
The cascade of unknown, remembered dreams;
The heaven-pointing spires of innocence;
The ribald rivalries of corniced wit;
The slopes of language, purpling the skies
Of doubt and jocularity and death. . . .
His restless mind has left no restless ghost
To haunt this alcoved suburb, where the past
Substantiates the insubstantial present:
Red bricked tradition stubbornly wedged
Between encroaching television masts;
Boys kicking football in the narrow park,
Caking their boots with the time-ridden clay;
Even this belly-banded bread-van horse:
Rattles the harness of a blinkered breed
That never cropped the grasses of Parnassus,

Or knows the sharp allurement of the spur
—And still weak sunshine titivates the Square.

Which is the traitor, then? — the artist, self-consumed
By silence, exile, cunning; haunted by
Creation's chimera? or the multitude,
Eating the gaudy lotus in the land
Whose hammocks are suspended in the past;
Where heroes are the order-of-the-day,
And artists Public Nuisances or fools?

# ARS POETICA

*(after P.K.)*

I am no match for knaves who've learned the trade
Of singing with a shilling in their mouth;
Whose tongues are silvered with a ready-made
Coating of minted syllables; my drouth
Is something bubbled Patronage can't slake.
I have no fake plethora of ideals
To toss, like any starving cur who'll shake
The paw with all who stroke its head, than steals
The larder's stock, and for further prey.
No, like a mute defiant ass, I munch
My Frugal nettlecrop of words, and bray
In outraged pride; stumble and stamp and crunch
The stones that pave the steep slopes to Parnassus,
Tweaked in the ear by prancing fools who clink
A silver bit — and whistle for Pegasus.

# LINES ON SITTING BEHIND A WELL-KNOWN POET ON A DUBLIN BUS

"A seat," I thought,
"And thirty separating years
Prism our cramped, intransigent identities;
Can I transcend the spectrum, and converge
Refractive idealities?
Seated in front, you saw, rainbow-suffused,
The dome-spread hills of Tempelouge approach;
And I, behind, sat watching through the drizzle
The variegated suburbs still encroach:
No terraced hierarchy for you to rail against;
No rounded myth for me to abrogate.
About us on the bus, with shrill bravura,
The blatant, cinemascopic world of schoolboys
Flaunted its wealth — imagination's booty;
Disdaining the lone prospectors' silhouettes,
 Panning for gold with frenzied eye and sinew
Between the crevices of mind and heart. . . .
Chastened — too near the terminus — I rued
(Anonymous, still perched behind your back)
How once I spurned your lapidary lore:
Here was implicit warranty, it seemed,
For our transverse insignia: that each must wear
Jointly and severally,
Mounting or alighting,
Intrepid or constrained,
Between the solemn city and bland hills,
His rue for ever with a difference.

# MAN AND WOMAN. . .

# DEIRDRE

Her skirt's soft swish made noiseless by the crack
Of saffron camp-fire flames where Naoise dozed,
Solemn as a kitten, she tiptoed
Nearer, and cupped her hands over his eyes,
Tinkling with laughter at his swift alarm.

Lightly enough he held her hand in his,
Fearing the brittle childhood in her eyes,
And boasted like a schoolboy; but his heart
Drummed loud decisions on his aching ribs,
And drained him of allegiance to the King.

Leaping like salmon over waterfalls,
Their love would shoot the rapids of pursuit
— So Deirdre said, persuading him they'd find
Refuge in Alba from King Conor's wrath,
Her words like summer breezes coaxing him.

They left at daybreak when the King was sleeping
Two stars in furtive combat with the dawn
Made Deirdre point excitedly; but he
Shivered and looked away, reminded suddenly
Of Conor's  cold eyes glinting like grey granite.

# REVOLUTIONS

Across the coffee-cups, our conversation spiralled,
Like cigarette-smoke from our smouldering thoughts,
And thoughts of thoughts the trained lips never uttered,
Intent on keeping the still-precious minute
Fondly wrapped up in swaddling platitudes.
The future dangled from the criss-crossed strings
Of vain conjecture, like a varnished puppet,
Mocking our sad, self-conscious fumbling:
With cords too numerous for us to master.
Promising, perhaps, an extra-special topple
To compensate our puzzled earnestness.

Oh, if I could unite those knots that fasten
You from me, darling, I would make a noose
Wide as the Equator; then, like Atlas, I
Would swing this spinning sphere above my shoulders;
Lasso the planet of my fixed desire;
And, like a jaunty child, discard my playthings.

# NOW, I MUST LIMP ALONE. . . .

Now, I must limp alone
The lonely road to where we started from,
When sapling mornings sprouted eagerness,
And splendid evenings beckoned in the distance,
Promising cool repose . . .
Why should I then lament
That cul-de-sac of grief
Now halt my heart's advance,
And cut off its retreat;
Or, sad somnambulist,
Night's camouflage still dare;
Groping for happiness,
Grasping the chasmed air?
For there were days before the sunlight hardened
When hours, demure as snowflakes and as gentle,
Lingered, oblivious of thudding time,
Bringing clear skies and peace;
Days that slipped by unnoticed, as the spring
Shapes imperceptibly the year's first rose,
Till suddenly she takes us unawares
In filigree perfection. . . .

I will remember how we laughed and talked,
Our quickened heart-beats measuring the night;
Your muted voice and the rare mystery
Of eyes as mild as honey, and as clear
As coral in unpenetrated seas
Where even sunlight startles;
I will remember all the cellophane
Of tenderness I wrapped about our world
To save it the evil finger-nails
That threatened suddenly, but my bandaged pride

Is cornered now, and baring its ugliness

Faces its penal servitude of grief,
Knowing the talked-of, last-minute reprieve
Is talked of only — or arrives too late,
Love's presence ousted by love's effigy.
And now good-morrow to our waking souls
which watch not one another out of fear.

# UPON O'CONNELL BRIDGE

Across the parapet we watched the sable river
Capture the city Lights, like grim inverted tapers
Brightening some underwater cavern
To eerie radiance.
Then suddenly you laughed, and the ffluorescent spell
Dissolved in the merriment that splashed
Whitely between your lips, and lightly in your eyes,
Making me happy, unaccountably.

What if these shining magpie days and nights
Sway in some future treachery of time,
Spilling their treasures on a world too sharp
For aimless happiness or laughter.
Let us snatch up each gesture and each phrase,
Each tinsel laugh for their own private values;
Building our stock-pile, not, as misers do,
For private gloating, but content to lean
Upon the parapet of each other's love;
Praying no dark and dreaded undercurrent
Will eddy its curling way into our lives.

# THE GLAZED HOUR

Sigh, slink or scurry in the glazéd hour,
Pale fugitive; weave the intricate skein
Of circumstance to cunning tapestries
To salve the guilty intellect and screen
The drab with shoddy unreality.

Her glance was passive as the sagging sky
Watching the panting leaves desert the tree,
That limp September evening, while the sun,
 Its summer's passion spent, haphazardly
Fondled the tinted residue.

Why should the shiver of a fretful leaf
Rasp, like a death-rattle? was it not kind
For us to part before some knowing wind
Severed this frail allegiance, etching our grief
Interminably in glazéd time?

# 'O, THERE CAN BE NO COMPROMISE'

O, there can be no compromise
Between deceit and truth;
Though yellow honey modifies
The aloe-bitter drouth.
The saturated tongue replies:
"O, there can be no compromise."

O, there can be no compromise,
My darling, we have failed
To keep love two-dimensional,
And now our reason's sailed
Adrift, beneath crouched, opaque skies,
Where there can be no compromise

O, there can be no compromise
When reason's in retreat,
Deceit will snuggle cosiest
Between truth's starched-white sheets:
But when the pennies seal our eyes
We cannot plead for compromise.

# LILAC WAS BRIGHTENING IN THE GARDEN

*(From the German of R. M. Rilke)*

Lilac was brightening in the garden;
The evening was filled with a prayer:
Parting, we left each other
Grief and despair.

Hot-tossed with dreams, the weary sun
Slipped from the hill's caress;
And now across dark-shadowing fields
Fades your white dress.

I see the shimmer gradually recede,
 And terror fills my mind;
Like a child staring fifixedly into a white light
— Now am I blind.

# IN THE DEVIL'S GLEN (Co Wicklow)

Here, in the valley, loveliness compels
Eyes upwards to the of trees,
Amber, and gold, and yellow with jet,
Crimson and unexpected violet.
Breathless we gaze, our excitement stretching
To snapping-point; until a timely cry
Of warning from a hidden bird distracts
Our glance elsewhere; then a snapping twig
Startles a squirrel to a clockwork ffight,
And beauty's tension eases in sudden laughter.
"Look," you exclaim, pointing to where an arch
Of tangled branches snares the slumping sun;
While we, unhampered, duck beneath the boughs
That beckon us to dappled happiness
Around the corner, and the next one, and the next . . .

Girl, in the depths of whose sequestered glance,
My aspirations focus, pray, o pray,
No note of bird, no trick-of-loop of season
May snare my faith or side-step my endeavour,
Making me party to the autumn's saraband,
Or victim to the winter's rampaging.

# AN EPİTAPH FOR UNBORN LOVE

Terse as a rifle-shot, this sniping doubt
Shatters the isolation of heart's eyrie,
Follows: the lethal ricochet of speech,
The evil landslide of disrupted truths.
Stillborn. love lies beneath recrimination's rubble

# PORTRAIT

Sitting together, we have known the truth:
The sunbeam hesitating through the window;
The anxious horse-hoof on the empty road;
The earnest conversation after silence,
That trickles like slow twilight through a room
Of lilac, turf-smoke, and an old-world portrait
Regarding us with private certitude
From a recess of the suspended past. . . .
Or is this half-truth only? was there not, too,
The hot sun pricking the responsive skin;
T he walk along the where the sea
Converged obliquely with the crimson sky,
Making an April evening deathless;
The clasp of conversation, and the glad embrace
Of loving — or of longing to be loved;
The sullen silence of the aftermath,
 As soul confronted soul's insolvency?

Let us be true to one another, love,
And true to our recessed identities;
Neither the neap nor ebb-tide of desire
Converges our refractive loneliness.
Let us be true: deciduous desire
Precincts a love entire and absolute,
The unremitting beacon of reality;
Let us be true without reproach or grief,
Seeing ourselves behind each other's guilt,
Shamefaced, but faithful to the mystery;
 Until, forgiven and forgiving all "
Our capsized passion flounders on the truth.

# THE WELL-SPRINGS

*(For Monessa)*

Seeking to isolate the victory
Of loving from the victory's defeat,
Men have gone mad, others committed suicide;
And others beat a tenuous retreat;
False reason baffled by its own deceit.

Dante, divine in anguish; Columbus, in regret,
Exploring new horizons of despair;
Swift, sanctifying anger, adroit Abelard,,
Thought they had smoked the devil his lair;
Still fifiendish laughter snivelled on the stair.

Let me take heart from other men's defeat;
Defy the spectre of the counterfeit:
Ransom the too-sharp ecstasy of taking;
Perceive another's thou; abide the self-forsaking
Abandonment of-giving; knowing love's course
Flows limpid if we purify the source.

# MAN AND NATURE . . .

# SPRING OFFENSIVE

Swift, spruce in battledress, the spring
Launches its offensive,
Taking the jaded winter unawares.
See, its defences crumble, as the barbed,
Bark barricades are tested and collapse;
Puffy and moist with sap, the helmeted
Spearheads of eager buds surge through the gaps.
 A spatter of shrapnel-sunshine, and a cat
Capitulates, and sprawls out readily;
And here, in No-man's-land, a sniping sparrow
Gobbles a worm, and jitterbugs in glee.

A nimble crocus, dodging the vicious thrusts
Of hostile winds, assails an open field
Alone, and, by a miracle, is left unscathed.
In the city, well-concealed
Behind their façades of indifference,
Hearts flutter, but the practised lips are mute,
When crimson gashes in an April sky
At evening implore a last tribute.
Ah, soon the summer's triumph will eclipse
The vibrant valour of the callow spring;
Behind the lines already it equips
Its forces for the final reckoning.

# FULL TIDE AND LANDSCAPE

Beneath the crouching headland the suave sea
Swaggers in arrogance, while the toady seabirds
Stagger and shriek with mealy-mouthed laughter
At every quip and gesture of the braggart,
Who wrings allegiance with cold tyranny.
But in this bay, a placid strip of coast
Rejects the sea's advances, and disdains
The glib effrontery of the dapper gulls,
Sleek in their well-groomed mediocrity.
Frothing in anger, the lascivious waves '
Whisper sly, tedious phrases of reproach;
Venture a little further; hesitate;
Then surge to their swift-swirling victory.
Frigid, impassive, the chaste stones clutch
Their cloistered virtue, disciplined as nuns,
Whose vow is their security which none
But they can violate ; shame may entreat,
But this calm dignity is consecrate.

Time passes, but oblivion delays;
Minutes, like poiséd gulls above the waves,
Uneasy, yet deliberate, somersault
Till all is consummated; and, abashed
By its most pyrrhic victory, the tide
Like any furtive tarquin slinks away.

# POEM IN LATE OCTOBER

From Kilmashogue, watching the evening sun
Shine on the city, making the factories
Gasometers and tenements appear,
Cleaned by a miracle of all ugliness,
"Isn't it just like summer," you exclaim.
And I agree, although we both know well
Enough that this delicious afternoon,
Filched from the summer, is a vagrant whim
Of Autumn, pouting for the gala days
Of dappled splendour: trees that bulged with song,
And grasshoppers that made the meadows loud;
Daisies spilt like milk on prudish lawns;
Poppies impatient of their stems' restraint;
And. fickle, lemon-coloured butterflies
Flirting at random with each gaudy flower..

But now the dusk blotches the patient sky
With violet bruises; soon the sun grows cold
And edges out of focus.
Somewhere a dog is barking, and the sound
Reproaches the still fields' indifference.
And later, coming down the hill we feel
The chill air tweeze our throats, reminding us
That sly November loiters round the comer,
Ready to reef the flimsy tegument
From Autumn's shoulders, leaving her bedraggled,
Waiting the shame of final nakedness.

# MAN AND GOD . . .

# THE SECOND TEMPTATION OF SAINT MARGARET OF CORTONA

Sadly, she watched the man who'd been her lover
Riveted in death; nothing to indicate
From his fixed features what eternal pain
Consumed his soul, or what eternal loss.
—Death's idiom can give a sinner's corpse
A mask as solemn as a halo'd saint's.
Her huddled thoughts in cowering agitation
Squatted on the flagstones of despair;
Passion's greedy flame-tongues licked no longer ;
Instead the lurid memory of sin
Slickered and smouldered, like a smoky wick
 Within the chill, dank vacuum of remorse,
That awful ante-room to Hell or Heaven.

"Despair is the loss of confidence in God."
Grace whispered swiftly, tugging at her heart; "
The well-spring of all virtue is His love;
He'll rinse the sin-bedraggled soul to whiteness,
As surely as He made the leper clean:
Then go, and sin no more" . . . . Satan replied:
This is presumption, for you are too great
A sinner to expect God's mercy; man's fate
Is moulded by environment, not Grace;
Then, since you're doomed already, never mind
The consequence of further evil; bind
Your hair up deftly, titivate your thee,
And robe yourself in your most daring gown;
Silk's rustle is an antidote to death
And you have beauty that can take men's breath

Away; keep sackcloth for a later day,
When blood is cool and passion impotent,
And it is twice as easy to repent;

But, for the moment, seek some other lord,
Who'll woo you with blithe praise and ornament,
And compensate you for your present loss."

"And will you damn another with yourself?"
Grace questioned quietly, knowing gentleness
Can soothe the soul that argument will tear
In shreds like tissue-paper; calmly, Margaret
Covered the dead man's deferential face
And knelt in prayer, each abject syllable
Grinding temptation's prism to smithereens.

# NO ROOM AT THE INN

*(From the German of Andreas Gryphus)*

The house is full;
There is no room
For you, or Her, or Him.
Why? Simply this:
We're full; crowded out.
 —Besides, the world itself
Is too narrow to contain
Him whom She contains.

# COUNTERPOINT

Love's periphery is more than loneliness,
Or thin circumference of finite pain
Bordering chaos; segments of compressed faith
In isolation, wedging the terrain
Of jagged truth from utter compromise
With rounded falsehood; taut temerity
Of longing for the centre's equipoise,
False radius of pride's dexterity.

There is another centre: fluorescent truths
Gliding like goldfish in the limpid sphere
Of vitreous desire and liquid reason,
Intact from time's caprice and probing fear.
Analogous, yet each unique in entity;
Reflecting love, projecting love's identity.